THE WALL STREET CRASH

29 OCTOBER 1929

Alex Woolf

Hodder
Wayland

an imprint of Hodder Children's Books

DAYS THAT SHOOK THE WORLD

Assassination in Sarajevo
D-Day
Hiroshima
Pearl Harbor
The Chernobyl Disaster

The Dream of Martin Luther King
The Fall of the Berlin Wall
The Kennedy Assassination
The Moon Landing
The Wall Street Crash

Produced by Monkey Puzzle Media Ltd
Gissing's Farm, Fressingfield
Suffolk IP21 5SH

First published in 2002 by Hodder Wayland
An imprint of Hodder Children's Books
Text copyright © 2002 Hodder Wayland
Volume copyright © 2002 Hodder Wayland

Series Concept: Liz Gogerly
Commissioning Editor: Alex Woolf
Editor: Jason Hook
Design: Jane Hawkins
Picture Researcher: Lynda Lines
Consultant: Michael Rawcliffe

Cover picture: An investor tries to sell his car after losing all his money in the stock-market crash (Corbis/Bettmann Archive).
Title page picture: Crowds in Wall Street following the stock-market crash on 24 October 1929 (Corbis/Bettmann Archive).

We are grateful to the following for permission to reproduce photographs:
AKG London 12, 21 (Erich Salomon); Alfred P Sloan, Jr/Museum Flint 30; Art Archive 8 top (Tate Gallery London/Eileen Tweedy); Associated Press 20 left; Bettmann Archive 23; Corbis 13 top (Library of Congress), 15 bottom (Underwood and Underwood), 27 Hulton-Deutsch Collection), 39 (Hulton-Deutsch Collection), 40 (Museum of the City of New York), 46 Bob Krist; Corbis/Bettmann Archive 7, 14, 16, 18, 20 right, 22, 24 top, 26 bottom, 28, 31 left and right, 32 bottom, 35, 36, 37 top and bottom; Mary Evans Picture Library 8 bottom, 26 top; MPM Images 24 middle; Peter Newark's American Pictures 9, 10 top and bottom, 29 bottom, 32 top, 33, 34, 38; Popperfoto 42 bottom (Mike Segar/Reuters), 43 (Peter Jones/Reuters); Topham Picturepoint 6, 11, 17 (UPI), 25, 41, 42 top. Artwork by Michael Posen.

Printed and bound in Italy by G. Canale & C.Sp.A, Turin

British Library Cataloguing in Publication Data
Woolf, Alex
The Wall Street crash. - (Days that shook the world)
1.Wall Street - Juvenile literature 2. Financial crises - New York (State) - Juvenile literature
I.Title
332.6'4273

ISBN 07502 3571 3

Hodder Children's Books
A division of Hodder Headline Limited
338 Euston Road, London NW1 3BH

CONTENTS

27 OCTOBER 1929: WALL STREET   6

MANIAS, PANICS AND CRASHES   8

THE JAZZ AGE   10

A MOOD OF OPTIMISM   12

THE MINI-CRASH   14

INVESTMENT TRUSTS   16

PRICES KEEP RISING   18

THE BABSON BREAK   20

24 OCTOBER 1929: BLACK THURSDAY   22

A NERVOUS RECOVERY   24

29 OCTOBER 1929: BLACK TUESDAY   26

HOW BAD CAN IT GET?   28

WHO WAS TO BLAME?   30

THE SLIDE INTO DEPRESSION   32

HOOVERVILLES AND THE BONUS ARMY   34

THE NEW DEAL   36

THE WORLDWIDE IMPACT   38

WHAT IF... ?   40

LEGACY   42

GLOSSARY, FURTHER INFORMATION   44

TIMELINE   46

INDEX   47

Crowds gather in the financial district of New York during the Wall Street Crash of October 1929.

O N A SUNDAY, WALL STREET, in the heart of the financial district of New York City, was usually as quiet as a graveyard. Yet on this Sunday, 27 October 1929, it was a hive of activity. Bankers, brokers and clerical assistants had given up their weekends and were in their offices struggling through mountains of work. Messenger boys hurried through the streets. Traffic police had lifted parking restrictions for the day, and dozens of cars filled Broadway, Broad Street, William Street and Wall Street itself. Sightseers gazed curiously at the Stock Exchange building, the centre of last week's dramatic stories of financial panic.

The streets were littered with pieces of 'ticker tape' – strips of paper displaying share prices. People could be seen picking these up and pocketing them like battlefield souvenirs. Tourist buses made special trips through the district and the conductors pointed out to the out-of-town passengers the Stock Exchange, 'where all that money was lost last week'. Restaurant owners, quick to see an opportunity, opened their doors. In the city's churches, preachers gave sermons about God punishing those who had lost sight of spiritual values through their single-minded pursuit of riches. It was the aftermath of a terrible week for the New York Stock Exchange.

For five years, the exchange on Wall Street had been at the centre of share-dealing on an incredible scale, involving hundreds of thousands of people across the USA. The more shares people bought, the more prices rose, and the more prices rose, the more people bought. This upward spiral had seemed unstoppable. Then, on Thursday 24 October, after a month of nervousness, a sudden fear had gripped the market. In a mad, chaotic scramble, people had begun to sell their shares, sending prices dropping through the floor.

No one could say for sure what had prompted this sudden panic, but by this Sunday almost everyone was certain that it was over. On Friday and Saturday, the banks had acted to calm the fear. Order had been restored, and the newspapers were full of the prospects for the following week. People believed that 'Black Thursday', 24 October, would be remembered as a blip, no more, in the history of the ever-rising market. Shares were again cheap, and there was bound to be a new rush to buy. As people went to bed on the Sunday evening, they could have little idea that the disaster, later known as the Wall Street Crash, had only just begun.

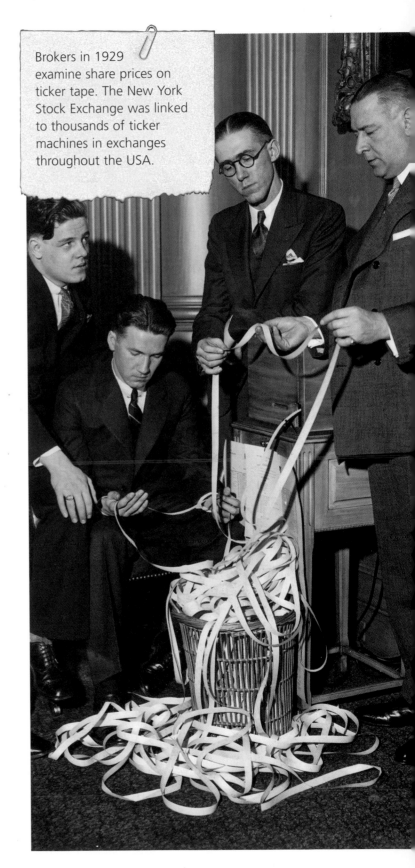

Brokers in 1929 examine share prices on ticker tape. The New York Stock Exchange was linked to thousands of ticker machines in exchanges throughout the USA.

The New York Stock Exchange

Shares are the many equal parts into which ownership of a company is divided. The New York Stock Exchange (NYSE) is the world's largest market-place for the buying and selling of these shares. It originated with a meeting of twenty-four brokers (people who buy and sell shares for other people) in 1792 under a buttonwood tree on what is now Wall Street. These brokers drew up a written agreement to deal only with each other. The NYSE was formally established in 1817.

Trading in London during the mania known as the South Sea Bubble.

IT IS PART OF HUMAN nature to be attracted by a money-making scheme, particularly if it seems to be making everybody else rich. The stock-market, where shares can be bought and sold at enormous profit, offers the ideal opportunity to follow this 'get-rich-quick' instinct.

People might hear about a promising new company, and then buy as many shares in it as they can afford – in the hope of benefiting from the expected rise in the shares' value. In the short term, with all this demand, the price of the shares might indeed rise, and everyone is happy. However, if demand keeps increasing, the price of the shares will be pushed up to a level out of all proportion to the actual value of the company that they represent.

This process is known as a mania, and is nearly always followed by the appearance of another very human instinct: panic. Panics occur when people suddenly lose faith in the value of the shares they hold, and decide, one after another, to sell. A rapid fall in prices, or 'crash', is the inevitable outcome.

A famous example of a mania was the South Sea Bubble. In 1720 the South Sea Company, a British business that traded with Spanish colonists in South America, reached an agreement with the British parliament to take over Britain's national debt (the amount of money the government owes). This was a vast sum of more than £30 million. In effect, the South Sea Company, collecting interest payments on the enormous debt, became banker to the British government. This led to a huge public demand for its shares, which rose more than 700 per cent in value in just seven months.

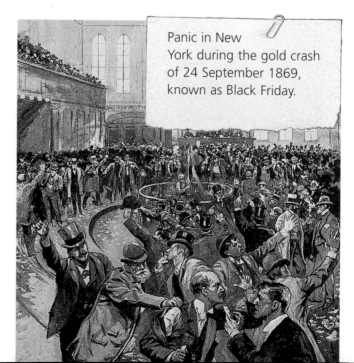

Panic in New York during the gold crash of 24 September 1869, known as Black Friday.

Those unable to buy South Sea shares were tempted by wily promoters into investing in new stock companies. Some of the ideas behind these companies were quite bizarre. They included trading in human hair, extracting silver from lead, producing a machine for making square cannonballs, and creating a wheel of perpetual motion. One company was proposed for 'an undertaking which in due time shall be revealed'. None of these companies ever traded, yet shares in all of them were snapped up by the eager public. But in September 1720, when news spread that directors of many of the new companies had sold their shares, there was panic and a general rush to sell. Prices collapsed, and a long economic depression followed.

The USA has also fallen prey to financial manias. In 1837 and 1857, for example, the American public was encouraged to invest in schemes to develop the infrastructure – especially the railroads – that would open up the American West. Again, people invested too heavily, and in 1873 over-speculation in the Northern Pacific Railroad led to a crash. Financial panic had also struck New York in 1869, following a rush to buy gold. When the government released its gold stocks for sale, prices dropped and thousands were ruined.

Tulipomania

During the early seventeenth century, Holland was gripped by a mania that reads like a fairy-tale. It was caused not by shares, but by tulip bulbs! A particular variety, infected with a virus that produced petals with coloured stripes, became all the rage. Tulip prices rose steadily as everyone, from nobles to servants, spent all their money on bulbs. The normal industry of the nation stopped. An entire house was traded for a single bulb. One sailor was thrown into prison after mistaking a tulip bulb for an onion, and eating it. Then one day the market simply ran out of buyers. Prices fell and panic set in. The economy plunged into a major depression.

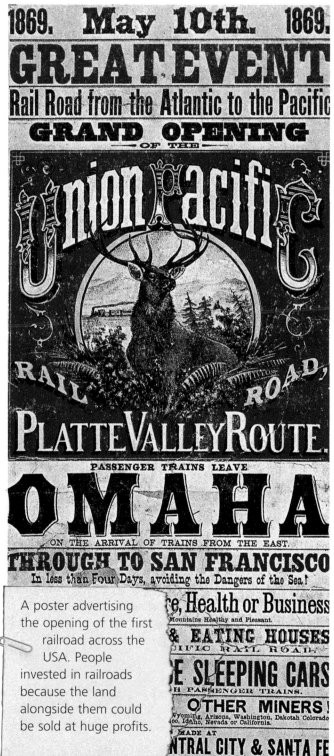

A poster advertising the opening of the first railroad across the USA. People invested in railroads because the land alongside them could be sold at huge profits.

9

The cover of *Life* magazine in 1928, showing the Charleston – one of the most popular dances of the 1920s.

I N THE USA, THE 1920s was a time of growing wealth and optimism. The First World War, which had ended in 1918, had been a conflict of unbelievable horror in which millions lost their lives. Many young, middle-class people reacted to this by turning their backs on traditional, more conservative, ways of behaving, and concentrating instead on having a good time.

It was the decade of Prohibition, when it was against the law to sell or consume alcohol. So, young Americans visited speak-easies – bars run by gangsters, where alcohol was sold illegally. The young, liberated women of the day were known as 'flappers'. They adopted a masculine look, styling their hair in a bob and smoking in public. It was also the decade of jazz music. Stars like Bix Beiderbecke, Louis Armstrong and Bessie Smith were giving new life and rhythm to popular music. They also gave the era its name: the Jazz Age. In the sporting world, it was a time of heroes. The baseball player Babe Ruth and the boxer Jack Dempsey were both more admired than the president.

In the 1920s, jazz music became popular all over the USA. One of its stars was Louis Armstrong, here playing trumpet with King Oliver's jazz band.

F Scott Fitzgerald, shown here with his wife and child, was one of the most famous writers of the 1920s. He invented the terms 'flapper' and 'Jazz Age'.

The Florida Land Boom

In 1925, everybody was getting rich in Florida buying and selling real estate. They believed that the bogs, swamps and scrubland would one day have value, just like the popular beachfront land. Buyers did not expect to live on the land – merely to sell it on at a profit. Then, in the autumn of 1926, two hurricanes killed 400 people, tore the roofs off thousands of houses and deposited tonnes of water and a few expensive yachts on the streets of Miami. The Florida Land Boom was over and thousands had lost all their money. With their optimism undiminished, many now turned to the stock-market.

Improvements in technology and production techniques led to cheaper consumer goods. Everyone wanted the latest high-tech product, whether it was a radio, a telephone, a refrigerator or, best of all, one of the new motor cars. The low cost of borrowing, and the willingness of banks to lend, meant that people could buy the latest status symbol even if they could not afford it. They simply paid it off bit by bit, using an 'instalment plan'.

Manufacturers were quick to realize the importance of advertising their products to the fashion-conscious and wealthy middle class. Adverts which appeared in the many new magazines and newspapers of the time were not government-controlled, and could make virtually any claim they liked. 'Try a Lucky, instead of a sweet!'

went a typical radio jingle – suggesting that Lucky cigarettes were non-fattening and therefore healthier. People were happy to buy the products and create for themselves the dream-world of the adverts: shining teeth, odourless breath, feet without corns, and trousers without wrinkles.

The introduction of new gadgets in the kitchen, and new food production techniques such as freezing and canning, meant fewer chores. People could now shop just once a week, and had more time to enjoy life. To afford their fun-filled new lifestyle, they still needed to earn money. But unlike earlier generations, they believed this could be done not by hard work, but by borrowing and investing. The easy credit terms offered by banks encouraged this 'get-rich-quick' state of mind.

Charles Lindbergh after his 33-hour flight across the Atlantic, for which he was awarded the Congressional Medal of Honor.

THE 1920s WAS A PERIOD of genuine prosperity for many Americans. Unemployment was low and production was high. Most workers saw their wages rise while prices remained stable. The exception to this were the farmers, who suffered from high costs and low prices for their goods. But for many people in the cities, things had never been better. The modern life that we now take for granted, with all its conveniences, was still a novel experience. People were ready to believe that money and technology were the answers to most, if not all, of the world's problems. There seemed no reason why the good times should not go on for ever.

The optimistic mood was illustrated by the achievement of the American aviator Charles A Lindbergh. On 21 May 1927, Lindbergh, in his aeroplane Spirit of St Louis, became the first person to fly solo, non-stop across the Atlantic, from New York to Paris. It was an age when anything seemed possible.

It was this mood of boundless optimism, this fascination with risk-taking, that led many people to start playing the stock-market – despite the recent memory of the Florida real estate crash. The stock-market offered a certain glamour, excitement, and of course the promise of wealth.

The companies people chose to invest in reflected the high-profile, booming industries of the time: General Motors (GM) for automobiles; Du Pont for high-tech products and popular new synthetic fabrics such as rayon and nylon; Wright Aeronautic for aeroplanes; and Montgomery Ward, a well-known retail and mail-order company. Most popular of all was Radio Corporation of America (RCA). RCA dominated the exciting new medium of radio communications, and was Wall Street's high-flying stock of the decade. In the five years prior to September 1929, prices rose from $11 to $114 per share.

During the boom days of the Twenties, the New York Stock Exchange was a very lively place to be. From 10 am, when a gong was struck to announce the start of trading, to 3 pm, when trading ceased, the exchange floor buzzed with activity. The favourite stocks and shares were traded at seventeen separate posts. These were horseshoe-shaped trading counters spaced over 1,400 square metres of floor, and each traded in different types of stock. The stock 'tickers', which recorded the changing share prices, were housed under glass domes. They were linked to thousands of similar tickers in stock exchanges and brokers' firms throughout the USA. Some 800 kilometres of tape ran over the spindles of each of these tickers for every million shares traded.

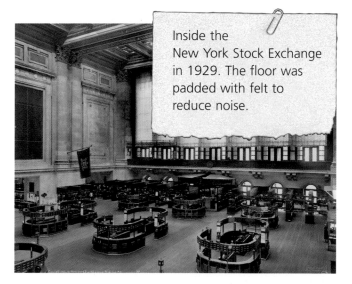

Inside the New York Stock Exchange in 1929. The floor was padded with felt to reduce noise.

Bulls and Bears

" O hush thee, my babe, granny's bought some more shares,
Daddy's gone to play with the bulls and the bears,
Mother's buying on tips and she simply can't lose,
And baby shall have some expensive new shoes. "

Anonymous song from the 1920s.

On the stock-market, bulls are traders who buy shares, hoping that the price will rise. Bears are traders who agree to sell shares, then try to buy them more cheaply before delivery. A bull market is one where share prices are rising. A bear market is one where share prices are falling.

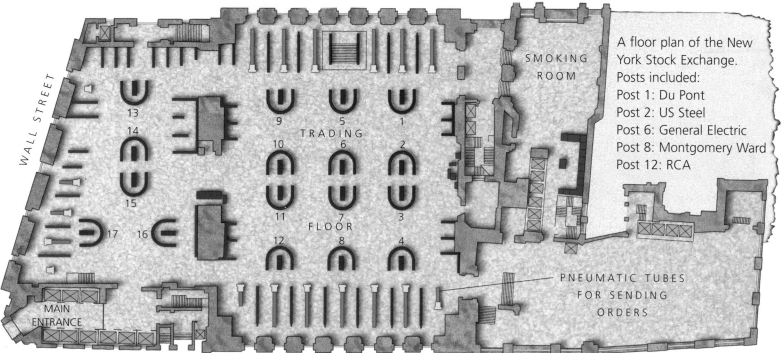

SMOKING ROOM

13
14
15
17   16

9   5   1
TRADING
10   6   2
11   7   3
FLOOR
12   8   4

WALL STREET

MAIN ENTRANCE

PNEUMATIC TUBES FOR SENDING ORDERS

A floor plan of the New York Stock Exchange. Posts included:
Post 1: Du Pont
Post 2: US Steel
Post 6: General Electric
Post 8: Montgomery Ward
Post 12: RCA

The St Valentine's Day Massacre, shown here in a police reconstruction, made all the headlines in February 1929.

ON 14 FEBRUARY, ST VALENTINE'S DAY, 1929, four gangsters disguised as policemen and working for Al 'Scarface' Capone burst into a garage on Chicago's North Side. There they gunned down seven men from the rival gang of George 'Bugsy' Moran. On the same day, the Federal Bank of New York decided at last to do something about the wild speculation in stocks and shares. They raised interest rates from 5 per cent to 6 per cent, to discourage people from borrowing so much money to buy shares. Unlike the St Valentine's Day Massacre, the bank's action did not make any headlines – in fact it was barely noticed by eager investors on Wall Street.

This was one of the few attempts by anyone in government or banking to curb the reckless behaviour of stock-market investors. Most people in authority fully supported what was happening on Wall Street. The Republican government followed a policy of laissez-faire, which meant letting things be. They did not believe in interfering with the natural movements of the stock-market. Leading bankers, captains of industry, journalists and academics were, almost without exception, delighted with the rising stock-market. They believed it reflected a healthy and expanding economy.

However, not everyone was blind to what was happening. The Federal Reserve Board (FRB), which monitored the nation's banking, was particularly worried by a recent increase in trading 'on margin'. This means buying shares by putting down a small deposit, then paying the balance later out of the profit made from the shares' rise in value. This form of trading worked very well, so long as the share prices kept going up!

In March 1929, the FRB held a series of secret meetings, which led to rumours of a steep rise in interest rates. People began to sell their shares. On 26 March, the hundreds of telephone clerks who sat in their cramped booths around the edge of the

The Industrial Average

In share trading, a point equals $1. If a company's shares rise 3 points, each share has risen $3 in price. The industrial average is the average value of shares in the top thirty companies on the Stock Exchange, and is a good indicator of the performance of the stock-market. The industrial average changed as a rule between 1 and 5 points per day. There were a few falls between 1924 and 1929, but most days ended with the prices higher than they were at market opening. At the end of 1924 the industrial average stood at 120 points. By the end of 1925 it had risen to 156. By the end of 1927, it stood at 202, and a year later, the average had reached 300.

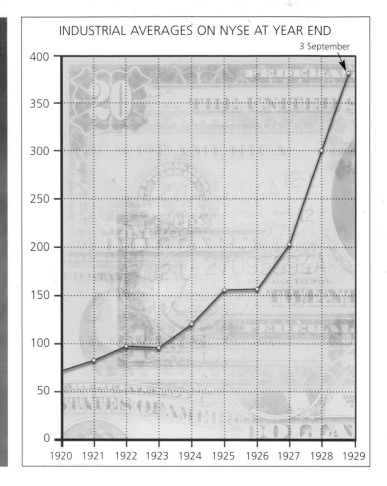

INDUSTRIAL AVERAGES ON NYSE AT YEAR END

3 September

Stock Exchange floor were suddenly swamped with orders to sell. They passed these orders to 'page boys', who inserted each slip of paper into a pneumatic tube. These tubes fired the orders to the appropriate post.

So much selling caused a fall that morning of 15 points in the 'industrial average' (see panel). In the afternoon, Charles E Mitchell, president of the National City Bank, the largest bank in the USA, calmed fears. He promised to keep his bank's interest rates low whatever the FRB decided, and loan money to whoever needed it. The mood of optimism was quickly restored. But the 'mini-crash' had shown that the boom was not, perhaps, as solid as it seemed.

The members of the Federal Reserve Board. Their daily Washington meetings in March 1929 led to the mini-crash.

William Crapo Durant, creator of General Motors, was one of the most powerful operators on Wall Street in the late 1920s.

So GREAT WAS THE STAMPEDE to buy shares in 1928 and 1929 that people began to fear the country might be running out of them. Shares in popular companies such as General Electric and RCA were in particularly short supply. An ingenious response was the introduction in the late 1920s of 'investment trusts' (ITs), which today are known as mutual funds. A typical IT held stock in 500 to 1,000 different companies. So, when people bought shares in the IT they were buying a stake in the profitability of a whole range of companies. The creation of ITs meant there was now almost no limit to the number of shares available.

ITs were created by other companies, such as banks. The fact that they produced nothing, and often had no offices or furniture, did not deter people in the slightest. They appeared to take the guesswork, and a lot of the risk, out of investing in stocks and shares. No longer did the amateur investor have to pore over the industrial average trying to calculate what was going up, and what was going down, before making his choice. ITs were managed by professionals – people with real financial wisdom. This was the age of hero-worship – from sports stars to aviators – and the men of finance were no exception. People were eager to share in the success of such financial giants as General Motors' William C Durant and John J Raskob.

During 1928, 186 ITs were launched. A further 265 appeared the following year. Shares in one IT, the Goldman Sachs Trading Corporation (GSTC), gained by over 100 per cent just three months after its formation in December 1928. So great was the demand that in the space of just five days in February 1929, the price of GSTC shares rose from $136 to $222. Speculation in these shares had pushed their value so high that they now represented a value of twice the total worth of the company's assets.

Customers in a stockbroker's office watch their personal wealth increasing with every new share price chalked up on the board.

This dangerous trend was occurring on a similar scale with many other ITs. The whole financial establishment – business leaders, investors, bankers, brokers – seemed to have lost touch with reality. It did not appear strange to them that share prices should be so high. After all, the prices represented not the current value but the future potential of companies. With so many talented people at the helm, investors believed this potential to be unlimited.

ITs were performing spectacularly well on a rising, or 'bull', market. When the Great Crash came, investors would discover ITs could perform just as spectacularly in reverse – shrinking to a fraction of their former value. Shares in GSTC, for example, would fall to $35 in October 1929. By 1932, they would be worth about $1.75.

Stock-Market Fever

" The rich man's chauffeur drove with his ears laid back to catch the news of an impending move in Bethlehem Steel; he held fifty shares himself on a twenty-point margin. The window-cleaner at the broker's office paused to watch the ticker, for he was thinking of converting his... savings into a few shares of Simmons. "

Frederick Lewis Allen, a contemporary observer, sums up the mass participation in the stock-market in 1929.

17

IN THE SPRING OF 1929, plans were drawn up for the construction of the Empire State Building, destined to be the world's tallest skyscraper. It was to be built in midtown Manhattan, some way north of Wall Street, where the money that financed the project had been made. John J Raskob, who commissioned the skyscraper, saw it as a permanent monument to 'the American way of life that allowed a poor boy to make his fortune in Wall Street'.

All that summer, as Raskob's hopes for the Empire State Building rose, so did prices on Wall Street. Increasing numbers of investors were attracted by the profits to be made in trading stocks and shares. People invested their life savings, mortgaged their homes or took out loans in the belief that here was a certain route to wealth. More than $7 billion had been loaned to investors by the end of the summer.

At this time, the stock-market dominated culture as never before. People who had shown no previous

Conceived during the boom and built after the crash, the Empire State Building took 7 million man-hours to complete and cost the lives of fourteen workers.

John Jakob Raskob (1879–1950)

John J Raskob was a leading businessman of the 1920s, and vice-president of General Motors (GM). He was one of several 'big men' of finance, whom the investing public believed had the power to raise or lower the market according to their will. In the case of Raskob, there may have been a grain of truth in this. In March 1928, on boarding a ship for Europe, he mentioned that GM stocks were cheap. Such was the magic of his name that GM stocks quickly soared from 187 to 199 points.

interest in Wall Street – actors, plumbers, seamstresses, speak-easy waitresses – would listen to the radio for tips on investment opportunities. The 'knowledgeable' amateur investor became the most prized guest at dinner parties, and his or her opinions were listened to with awe. Stories circulated that a broker's valet had made nearly a quarter of a million dollars on the market, and a nurse had made $30,000 simply by following tips given to her by grateful patients. A waiter at the Stock Exchange's luncheon club resigned his job $90,000 richer, as a result of advice passed on by customers.

Speculation became a full-time activity for many, and brokers' offices were crowded with customers from 10 am until 3 pm. The ticker service went nationwide,

bringing news of share prices for the cost of a local telephone call.

It was not only men who played the market. An article in the *North American Review* reported: 'Women have become important players of man's most exciting capitalistic game and the modern housewife now reads, for instance, that Wright Aero is going up… just as she does that fresh fish is now on the market.' In a private suite of the Waldorf Astoria Hotel – soon to be demolished to make way for the Empire State Building – a share-trading club for women was established. A dozen customers would recline there in comfort, smoking Turkish cigarettes in long holders, their eyes never leaving a screen that showed the changing prices.

Women check the ticker in 1929. Women outnumbered male shareholders in one company, Pennsylvania Railroad, so earning it the nickname the 'Petticoat Line'.

Baseball player Babe Ruth was the greatest sports star of the 1920s. His 1927 record of sixty home runs in a season lasted until 1961.

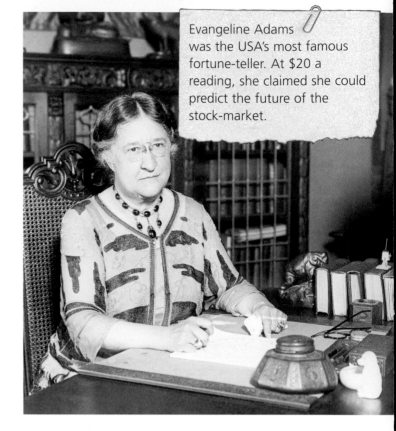

Evangeline Adams was the USA's most famous fortune-teller. At $20 a reading, she claimed she could predict the future of the stock-market.

THERE WAS NOTHING ESPECIALLY unusual about 3 September 1929. New York City was sweltering under a late summer heat wave. The papers reported that Babe Ruth had struck forty home runs so far that season, and the German airship *Graf Zeppelin* was nearing the end of its round-the-world flight. The astrologist Evangeline Adams, when asked for her opinion of the stock-market, replied: 'The Dow Jones (the industrial average) could climb to heaven'. And so it seemed to thousands, as the stock-market broke new records. No one could have known that 3 September would mark the high point of the 1920s bull market. Such prices would not be seen again for another twenty-five years.

Two days later, the economist Roger Babson addressed the Annual National Business Conference. He said: 'Sooner or later a crash is coming, and it may be terrific... factories will shut down... men will be thrown out of work... the vicious circle will get in full swing and the result will be a serious business depression.' There was a dip in the market in response to Babson's speech. The industrial average fell by 10 points, but had recovered by the next day.

This dip became known as the 'Babson Break'. People at the time thought it was just another of those little setbacks that frequently marked the continuing climb of the market. However, for those who wished to see them there were clear signs that the end was coming. By autumn 1929, the American economy was in recession. Manufacturing production had slowed down, and fewer houses were being built.

On Saturday 19 October the market experienced a heavy fall. Over 3 million shares were traded, and the industrial average fell by 12 points. A few 'margin calls' were sent out. This meant that stock held on margin had fallen in value so far that it could no longer be used as a guarantee that the loan used to buy it would be repaid. So, more money was demanded from the investor.

The early days of the following week were very worrying. There was a high volume of trade, and the ticker fell behind in printing the latest prices. So, people around the country often did not know how much they had lost until hours later. The industrial average fell to the level of the previous June, wiping out all profits that had been made since then.

Respected opinion on Wall Street insisted that this was merely a hiccup. Nevertheless, thousands went to bed on the evening of Wednesday 23 October thinking it might be better to cut their losses the following day, and sell all their shares.

Respected Opinion

" The industrial condition of the United States is absolutely sound. "

Charles E Mitchell, 15 October 1929.

" Stock prices have reached what looks like a permanently high plateau. "

Irving Fisher, Professor of Economics at Yale University, 15 October 1929.

Shareholders in a San Francisco hotel watch helplessly as share prices tumble. Similar scenes were taking place all around the country.

24 October 1929:
Black Thursday

AT 10.03 AM ON 24 OCTOBER 1929 the market opened 'like a bolt out of hell' according to one witness. Huge blocks of shares were bought and sold, but prices remained steady at first.

10.25 am A block of 20,000 General Motors shares was offered at a loss of 80 cents a share. Prices began to fall. A hysterical caller shrieked, 'Sell at the market!' This meant accepting any price offered. It became a common cry as prices accelerated downwards.

11.00 am The Stock Exchange floor was full of people desperate to sell. No one would bid for some shares. This created 'air holes' – very steep drops in prices – before a buyer could be found.

11.30 am Panic reigned on the market floor. At Post One, brokers were literally being pinned against the trading counter by the hysterical crowd. At Post Two, the price of Steel stocks was plunging by the minute, dragging other

Wall Street on 24 October 1929. A journalist described the scene: 'An enormous murmuring crowd. People pressed close around were talking… almost in whispers. Every now and then you could hear quite distinctly a hysterical laugh.'

stocks down with it. At Post Four, a fat, perspiring man was yelling orders that made no sense. He was seized and led away, and the Stock Exchange visitors' gallery was closed.

Pedestrians passing along Broad Street were startled by the sound of a strange roar coming from within the white walls of the Stock Exchange. A crowd gathered. Rumours spread that the market was in free fall. High up on one of the buildings, a workman climbed out to make some repairs. The crowd assumed he was a ruined investor preparing to commit suicide. They waited for him to jump.

11.50 am The latest prices were now fifty-five minutes late in being printed on the ticker tape. Around the country, people could no longer be certain of the prices coming off the ticker, and fear and ignorance led more and more to sell their shares.

12.00 pm A meeting was held between senior bankers, who established a $50 million pool to steady the market. This was known as 'organized support'. Word of the meeting spread to the exchange floor, and had an immediate effect. Prices stopped falling.

1.30 pm Richard Whitney, vice-president of the Stock Exchange, appeared on the floor. He walked up to Post Two and bid for 10,000 shares in Steel at $205 per share – 10 points higher than the price of the last sale. For a moment there was silence, then a cheer broke out. Whitney marched from post to post placing further big orders. Fear vanished from the traders' faces, giving way to anxiety that a new opportunity might be missed. Buying began again in earnest, and prices soared.

The recovery on Black Thursday was almost as remarkable as the crash that had come before it. The industrial average closed at 299, only 12 points down from the previous day's close.

The trading floor of the New York Stock Exchange on a typical boom day in 1929.

A Personal Loss

" The Mount Vernon police reported last night that none of the relatives or friends of Abraham Germansky, a real estate broker of 140 East Broadway, New York, who disappeared on Thursday, had seen or heard from him. After the crash in stocks of that day Germansky was seen walking up Broadway tearing up ticker tape. His friends believe he lost considerable money on Thursday and that his loss affected his mind. "

The New York Times,
28 October 1929.

Investors jostle to read a newspaper reporting the losses of Black Thursday. The *New York Times* declared: 'Wall Street optimistic after stormy day.'

The New York Times

Friday, October 25, 1929

WORST STOCK CRASH STEMMED BY BANKS; 12,894,650-SHARE DAY SWAMPS MARKET; LEADERS CONFER, FIND CONDITIONS SOUND

ON BLACK THURSDAY, A RECORD 12,894,650 shares had been traded. The Stock Exchange clerks worked through the night to process all the transactions. Thousands listening in around the country received news of the recovery when it was too late and they had already sold all their shares. Many had mortgaged their houses and spent all their savings on the promise of wealth. Now they had nothing. The most bitter part of it was the realization that they might have held on to their homes, their cars and their dreams of a better life had they not sold their shares during the panic.

Over the next few days, a joint effort was made by bankers, business leaders and politicians, including the

American president Herbert Hoover, to steady people's nerves. Everyone said the economy remained sound, the crisis was over, and it was back to business as usual. Evangeline Adams, the astrologer, told all her clients that the market would witness a substantial swing upwards – then informed her broker to sell all her shares first thing tomorrow.

On Friday and on Saturday (when a morning session was always held) trading was heavy, but confidence held and prices remained quite steady. Banks and investment houses bought up large chunks of stock to help reverse the losses of the previous week. The *Wall Street Journal* called what had happened a 'panic'. It said those who owned stock outright rather than on margin should remain confident: 'They have lost a few tail feathers but in time they will grow again, longer and more luxurious than the old ones.'

But the nerves of thousands of investors had been shredded. On Sunday evening, they must have decided that enough was enough. Monday 28 October opened with a flood of selling which swept the market off its feet. And this time there was no rally. Organized support did not appear at noon like the cavalry on the horizon. The bankers had perhaps become aware of their own impotence in the face of a frenzied desire to sell.

The industrial average had fallen from 299 to 261 by the time the bell sounded at the close of business. Less shares had been traded than on Black Thursday, but the market had fallen three times further.

Some $10 billion had been wiped off values on the New York Stock Exchange alone. This was the largest drop in prices during any day in the exchange's history. And the biggest falls had occurred in the last few minutes of trading – an extremely bad omen for the next day's opening.

A Moment in Time

At 6.30 pm, Monday 28 October 1929, New York bankers release a chilling statement to the press. They say it is not their responsibility to maintain any level of prices or protect anyone's profit. Their only aim is to maintain order in the market so that offers are met by bids at some price. It is little comfort to investors to hear that their dreams will be allowed to die, but they will be given an orderly funeral.

One o'clock in the morning on 25 October, and Wall Street brokers phone their clients requesting more margin.

Panic at the Stock Exchange. Shares which had cost people their life savings were being sold for a fraction of their value.

BLACK TUESDAY, 29 OCTOBER 1929, was the worst day of the Great Crash. It is remembered now as the most infamous day in the history of Wall Street.

10.00 am The Stock Exchange superintendent struck the gong to signal the start of the day's trading. The sound was lost in the din. 'Twenty thousand Steel. Sell at the market!' 'Thirty thousand – sell!' At all seventeen trading posts, large blocks of stock were dumped on the market for whatever price they could get. It was clear from the size of these blocks that today it was the millionaires who were panic-selling. Most of the small investors had already been wiped out by the crashes on Thursday and Monday.

At Post Seventeen, men were literally charging into the crowd in an effort to sell shares in Telephone and Telegraph. One broker lost his false teeth while shouting an order and was nearly trampled underfoot as he went searching for them. At Post Twelve, RCA shares, once worth $420 each, were now selling for $26. At Post Four, where shares in Anaconda Copper were quickly plummeting, a middle-aged, collarless broker with a tear in his jacket, emerged from the crowd moaning: 'I'm sold out! Sold out!'

Mounted police restore order on Wall Street, where there had been commotion following news of the crash.

Richard Whitney, the hero of Black Thursday, was being pushed and shoved like everyone else. Within half an hour, three and a half million shares had been sold for a combined loss of over $2 billion.

11.00 am Brokers were seen in tears. Men kneeled in prayer at the edge of the exchange floor. Some went to the nearby Trinity Church where, for the first and perhaps only time, Protestants, Catholics and Jews prayed together.

12.00 pm The senior bankers met. Far from offering organized support, a rumour went round that they were actually selling stocks. For ordinary investors this news was like seeing the crew of a sinking ship elbowing passengers aside to get to the lifeboats. The reputation of the bankers was ruined.

2.55 pm As trading drew to a close, a few brokers raised their hands and began bidding for stocks. Finally, prices began to rally.

3.00 pm The closing gong rang. The shouting stopped. Slowly, dejectedly, the brokers left the floor. The porters began to sweep up the torn ticker tape, which littered the floor like a thick carpet. The industrial average was down an astonishing 43 points to 230 – back to the level of November 1928. The volume of sales – 16,410,030 shares in all – broke all records. And it could have been even worse, but for the small rally before the close.

A Moment in Time

At 1 pm, 29 October 1929, ten thousand people fill Wall Street, from Broadway to the Hudson River. Rumours pass up and down the crowd. No one knows what to believe, or how to behave. Nothing like this has ever happened before. All over the city, people stand in groups watching the glass bowls in which spools of ticker tape unwind. The falling numbers show the tumbling share prices, and tell tales of shrinking fortunes. Some people want to talk about how much they have lost, but nobody wants to listen. It is too common a story.

A telephone operator at a share-buying club writes up the latest prices as they come in from New York. On Black Tuesday, news of prices fell behind by up to two and a half hours.

On Black Tuesday, over $14 billion had been wiped off the value of the stock-market. By way of comparison, the entire budget of the American government in 1929 was $3 billion. In one day, the USA had lost more money than it had spent in the whole of the First World War. But this was still just the beginning. What made the 1929 crash worse than any other, before or since, was the way the market kept falling – day after day, week after week, month after month.

If someone had deliberately set out to lead as many people as possible into financial ruin, they could not have planned it any better. The small-time investors had been wiped out early on. The bigger players had soon followed. Even the clever ones who waited until December to buy shares at what seemed like bargain prices, would see their value drop by a third over the next two years.

By mid-November 1929, the industrial average stood at 224 points, half of what it had been on 3 September. June 1930 saw another large drop. It continued its sickening slide for two more years, reaching an ultimate low of 41 points in July 1932.

Between one million and three million Americans were immediately and directly affected by the crash. Many of them were bankrupted. Thousands of families, whose cars, furniture and jewellery had been bought with instalment plans, had to watch as their possessions were taken away. Husbands and wives discovered with horror that their partners had been using their savings to play the market.

Sign of the times: a bankrupt investor tries to raise cash by putting his car up for sale.

There were some high-profile casualties. William Crapo Durant, founder of General Motors, lost $40 million in the crash. In 1936, he declared himself bankrupt, listing his total assets as $250 worth of clothing. John J Raskob lost several million, but survived to live comfortably and see his Empire State Building become a famous part of the Manhattan skyline. J P Morgan, the famous banker, lost somewhere between $20 million and $60 million, while Michael Meehan of Radio Corporation of America, who had speculated heavily in his own stock, lost approximately $40 million.

Some ruined speculators committed suicide. The head of Rochester Gas and Electric Company gassed himself. Another investor escaped from his margin calls by pouring petrol on himself and setting it alight. On the Saturday following the crash, the body of a businessman was fished out of the Hudson River. His pockets contained $9.40 in change, and some margin calls.

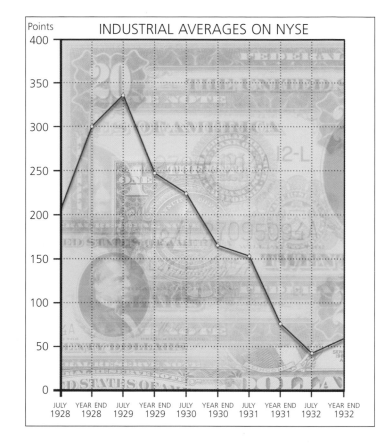

INDUSTRIAL AVERAGES ON NYSE

| Points | JULY 1928 | YEAR END 1928 | JULY 1929 | YEAR END 1929 | JULY 1930 | YEAR END 1930 | JULY 1931 | YEAR END 1931 | JULY 1932 | YEAR END 1932 |

A cartoon of suicidal brokers from November 1929.

Black Humour

On 30 October 1929, John D Rockefeller, the 90-year-old founder and owner of Standard Oil and one of the richest men in the world, declared:

" Believing that the fundamental conditions of the country are sound… my son and I have for some days been purchasing sound common stocks. "

Eddie Cantor, a comedian and stock-market victim, replied:

" Sure, who else had any money left? "

IT WAS NATURAL AFTER THE trauma of the crash that people would search for someone to blame. In Washington, the Democratic Party was highly critical of the Republican president, Herbert Hoover. They claimed that his laissez-faire policies had allowed the crash to happen. Hoover's popularity began to plummet, and he would be convincingly defeated by Franklin D Roosevelt in the 1932 presidential election.

The headquarters of the Union Industrial Bank in Flint, Michigan, which in 1929 was the scene of the world's biggest bank fraud. A group of employees stole $3.5 million of customers' money, and lost it all on the stock-market.

A Senate committee was set up to investigate Stock Exchange practices. This exposed some of the controversial behaviour of banks and traders, and led to changes in the law. One practice that would be made illegal was 'market-rigging' – the manipulation of share prices for personal profit. It had been quite common for large-scale traders to try to entice small-time speculators into buying shares in a certain company by buying a block of shares themselves. The share price was then driven up, and they could sell their block for a substantial profit. Another way of market-rigging was to spread a rumour that a certain stock was about to rise in value, often by bribing journalists to write a favourable report.

Economics experts, who had been so optimistic in their predictions about the market, were criticized. Yale's Professor Irving Fisher made some unconvincing attempts to explain his miscalculations:

Richard A Whitney (1888–1974)

Richard Whitney, vice-president of the New York Stock Exchange, borrowed heavily in the years before and after the crash in order to purchase stock in his own company. This policy worked so long as prices were rising. But after the crash, his shares fell below a value sufficient to act as guarantee for these loans. As his position became desperate, he began using shares belonging to other people as guarantees for his loans. By 1938, no bank was willing to lend him money, and he was forced to visit the most casual of acquaintances to borrow funds. Finally, he was suspended from the Stock Exchange for bankruptcy.

'It was the psychology of panic. It was mob psychology, and it was not, primarily, that the price level of the market was unsoundly high.' But the professor's reputation, like so many others, had been dented by the crash. The *Commercial and Financial Chronicle* commented: 'The learned professor is wrong as he usually is when he talks about the stock-market.'

The bankers and investment companies most associated with the speculation on Wall Street also received stinging criticism. Several high-profile individuals were singled out, including Charles E Mitchell who had appeared so heroic in the mini-crash of March 1929. Mitchell had speculated extensively in the stock of his own National City Bank. In the week beginning 28 October 1929, he had tried to reverse the sudden decline in the worth of this stock by borrowing $12 million from another bank and using it to buy even more National City stock. Mitchell learned to his cost the difficulties of supporting a stock when everyone else wants to sell. National City shares fell from 500 to 200 points by the end of the year, and Mitchell ran out of money. He resigned in March 1933, and was later arrested for tax evasion.

The economist Irving Fisher had said that the market would get stronger after it absorbed the good effects of Prohibition, which had made the American worker 'more productive and dependable'. Three days later, Wall Street crashed.

Charles E Mitchell (right) following his arrest for income tax evasion. He was eventually able to repay his debt to the government in 1938.

31

The Great Depression affected rich and poor alike. Here, in 1931, a former businessman is reduced to selling apples on a street corner.

UNEMPLOYED
BUY AN
A[...]

IN THE TEN YEARS THAT followed the crash, the USA and the rest of the world suffered a massive and prolonged economic slow-down known as the Great Depression. By 1932 in the USA, there were 14 million people out of work and many businesses were bankrupt. The forced closure of many American banks involved in stock-market speculation led the USA to recall loans it had made to Europe and elsewhere. The depression spread in this way around the world. Unemployment soared to 6 million in Germany and 3 million in Britain.

The severity of the Great Depression threw Americans into a state of shock. Some saw it as the fulfilment of a medieval prophecy. Others claimed it was divine justice for the self-indulgence and greed of the 1920s. President Hoover blamed the weak economies of Europe, stating: 'The European disease had contaminated the United States.'

During the 1930s, soup kitchens like this one opened up all over the USA to help feed those most affected by the Great Depression.

Most people, however, believed that the Wall Street Crash of October 1929 had been the trigger for the Great Depression. But is there any evidence to suggest that the crash led directly to the depression?

An economic recession was certainly on its way in 1929, with or without the crash. Improvements in technology had meant that, for several years, American farmers and manufacturers had been producing more goods than they could sell. This had led to a decline in industrial production by the summer of 1929.

The crash did, though, make this poor economic situation very much worse. The wealth of the USA in the 1920s was very unevenly shared. Sixty per cent of Americans remained on incomes at or below the level necessary for basic living. The consumer boom in radios, cars and household appliances was enjoyed by only a minority of wealthier citizens, and there were not enough of them to sustain such big increases in manufacturing. The crash, when it came, affected this wealthier sector more than any other – and the economy depended most on their money for its continued health. As the wealthy members of society suffered, so did the economy.

Popular songs of the day reflected the change in the national mood from optimism to despair. In 1930, people hopefully sang *Happy Days Are Here Again*, but the national income dropped from $87 billion to $75 billion. In 1931, a popular song was *I've Got Five Dollars*, and the national income fell to $59 billion. It declined to $42 billion in 1932, and the country's desperate mood was captured perfectly by the words of *Brother, Can You Spare a Dime?*

During the Great Depression, drought turned the central USA into a 'dust bowl'. Here, in May 1936, a car and farm machinery are buried by dust at Dallas, South Dakota.

A Moment in Time

On Sunday 14 April 1935, the day is warm with a gentle breeze whispering out of the south-west. Suddenly, a black cloud appears on the horizon. Birds fly ahead of it, but it is travelling at nearly 100 kilometres per hour and they cannot escape its fury for long. People stay in their houses, wedging cloths in the cracks of doors and windows, and tying handkerchiefs over their faces. The dust storm turns day into night, and people believe the world is coming to an end.

This is one of many storms that for three years have plagued Texas, Oklahoma, Kansas and Colorado. The region, which has suffered the worst period of droughts, dirt storms, tornadoes and floods in its history, has become known as the 'dust bowl'. This environmental disaster has arrived at the same time as the terrible economic depression which has driven down crop prices and destroyed the livelihoods of many rural people.

DURING THE 1928 PRESIDENTIAL campaign, Herbert Hoover had said: 'We are nearer today to the ideal of the abolition of poverty and fear from the lives of men and women than ever before in any land.' One year later, the stock-market crash had plunged the USA into the worst economic collapse in its history.

It is quite likely that, had the crash and the Great Depression not occurred, Hoover would have been remembered as a successful president. He was certainly popular until 1930. But when the depression hit, he failed to act effectively to provide relief for people's suffering, or to appear as if he even cared. Hoover believed in 'rugged individualism'. It was his view that people should look after themselves, and not rely on the government for support.

Hoover resisted demands for relief payments to be made to the poorest sections of the population. He believed such payments would weaken the people's will and make them too dependent on the government.

HOOVERVILLE

"IT SEEMS THERE WASN'T ANY DEPRESSION AT ALL!"

This 1930s cartoon sums up the popular view of Hoover as an uncaring president, removed from the reality of people's suffering.

Hoover also believed in a balanced budget, and was unwilling to introduce a welfare programme that would put the government into debt. This was unfortunate because at this time higher spending was exactly what was needed, to relieve the suffering of so many unemployed and to increase consumer demand.

Many of the unemployed had lost their homes, and were forced to live on the streets. They began forming huge shanty towns on the edges of cities. Some people made their homes in shacks constructed from orange boxes. One family lived in a box that a grand piano had been delivered in. The homeless started calling these shanty towns 'Hoovervilles' after a president who they believed was doing little to help them. Eventually, in 1932, Hoover approved a policy of lending money to states for relief purposes. But this small-scale programme did little to help the suffering of the poor, or to stimulate economic recovery.

In the summer of 1932, thousands of poor First World War veterans, calling themselves the Bonus Army, arrived and set up camp in Washington DC.

The veterans had been promised a bonus payment, but it was not due until 1945. They had come to pressure Congress into bringing it forward. Hoover, who was against paying the bonus and concerned at the danger to public order, sent in troops under General Douglas MacArthur to drive off the veterans.

After MacArthur's action, Hoover's popularity nose-dived. He lost the 1932 election to the Democratic candidate Franklin D Roosevelt.

A Moment in Time

At 4 pm, 28 July 1932, American troops led by General Douglas MacArthur advance down Pennsylvania Avenue, Washington DC. They herd the veterans of the Bonus Army away from a camp of huts and tents, and set it ablaze. By 8 pm the downtown area is cleared. Hundreds have been injured by tear gas, bricks, clubs, bayonets and sabres. Ignoring Hoover's instructions, MacArthur sends his troops across the bridge to set light to the Bonus Army's main camp on the other side of the Anacostia River. A sad stream of veterans, along with 600 women and children, are forced to leave behind their makeshift homes.

Bonus Army marchers in Washington are dispersed by soldiers with tear-gas. Ten thousand veterans were cleared from their camp by the day's end.

President Roosevelt used radio to transmit his famous 'fireside chats'. His great skill was his ability to explain his policies simply and clearly to the American people.

WHEN ROOSEVELT BECAME PRESIDENT on 4 March 1933, the Great Depression was at its height. More than 16 million people were unemployed and the American banking system had collapsed. Roosevelt realized he had to act both to relieve the suffering of the poor and unemployed, and also to bring about an economic recovery. He did not have any magical answers, but Americans were accepting of a president more willing to experiment than the inflexible Hoover.

The New Deal was the name given to a whole range of programmes introduced by Roosevelt to lift the USA out of the depression. In the first year of his administration, Roosevelt introduced measures to get people spending money again – by making businesses agree to pay fair wages and charge fair prices. He helped the farmers by setting up the Agricultural Adjustment Administration, which bought up surplus crops and paid farmers to reduce production. This raised prices for their products. To help solve the problem of unemployment, Roosevelt set up massive public works projects, building schools, courthouses, bridges and dams. This created employment for many thousands of people. Meantime, the Social Security Act of 1935 provided much needed welfare payments for the unemployed, and retirement benefits for older American workers.

Roosevelt was also responsible for major changes to the structure of the US economy. The banking system, weakened by the 1929 crash, was in urgent need of reform. A law was passed to safeguard those with small savings against losing all their money if the banks closed. It ensured that banks did not speculate in their own stock as they had done so irresponsibly in 1929.

WPA workers widening a street. The WPA did not just provide jobs. Many of its projects were of lasting benefit to local communities.

Some New Deal Agencies

The Civilian Conservation Corps (CCC) provided work in the countryside, clearing wasteland and planting forests. Four million people were given temporary work.

The Works Progress Administration (WPA) built and repaired new roads, public buildings, libraries, hospitals and schools.

The Tennessee Valley Authority (TVA) helped to revitalize one of the most depressed areas of the country by building dams to provide electric power and control flooding.

The National Recovery Administration (NRA) encouraged employers to pay fair wages and accept trade unions.

Joseph Kennedy, the first chairman of the SEC. Kennedy, a wealthy Wall Street speculator, was said to have indulged in the very practices the SEC was set up to prevent.

The law also increased the power of the Federal Reserve Board to control banking activity and stop people trading on margin if it chose. In 1934, the Securities and Exchange Commission (SEC) was established to police the stock-market and make sure that none of the shadier practices of the late 1920s, such as market-rigging, reappeared.

To help the homeless, Roosevelt's government set up the US Housing Authority to knock down slums and build low-cost housing. The Home Owners Loan Corporation was established to offer people the finance to buy homes without the risk of having them seized by the banks.

The New Deal brought relief, employment and housing to millions of people. However, a general economic recovery was a long time coming, and the Great Depression ground on through the 1930s. It did not fully end until 1941, when the USA entered the Second World War.

Another bank closes in Germany. In July 1931, a rush to withdraw money forced the government to close all banks for several weeks.

THE RIPPLES CAUSED BY the Wall Street Crash were felt all around the world. During the boom years of the 1920s, American banks had loaned vast amounts of money to European countries to help stimulate their economies after the devastation of the First World War. When American businesses began to fail after the crash, the USA was forced to call in these loans. This had disastrous consequences for European economies.

To make matters worse, the USA raised import taxes drastically, to help its own industries by making goods from abroad more expensive. This prompted similar measures by European countries. The result was a drop in world trade, and huge rises in unemployment. In Britain, a quarter of the workforce was unemployed by the spring of 1931. In Denmark, the depression reduced the industrial workforce by a staggering 40 per cent.

Germany was the worst hit. It had relied on American loans not only to rebuild its economy after the First World War, but also to pay reparations (compensation for war damages) to the victorious nations. As the depression hit, industrial production in Germany slumped, falling by almost half, while a fifth of the working population became jobless in the space of three years between 1930 and 1933.

As the economic crisis spread, there was growing social and political unrest. In many parts of Europe there was increasing dissatisfaction with democracy, and a move towards political extremism. Communists predicted the end of capitalism. Fascists tried to channel people's anger into an aggressive nationalism, and blamed 'foreigners' such as the Jews for the economic woes. As people became more desperate, they became more and more willing to listen to such extreme solutions.

In 1929 in Germany, the fascist National Socialist Party, or Nazis, had just 170,000 members. But after the economic chaos caused by the Wall Street Crash, the Nazis began to grow into a truly national movement. By 1932, they had over a million members. The Nazis were able to use the misery of mass unemployment to gain support in general elections. In January 1933 their leader, Adolf Hitler, became chancellor of Germany. The consequences for the world would be devastating.

International relations were under strain because of the hardships of the depression. Tensions rose and countries began to rearm. Foreign policy became more aggressive, especially in Germany, Italy and Japan. The world was heading for another war.

Adolf Hitler

" Hitler was now a factor to be reckoned with. He claimed some half a million followers, and more were joining the Party every day. His rallies in Bavaria and the Rhineland attracted large crowds. Hitler had never yet referred specifically to the economic policies he planned for Germany, although he frequently criticized the 'Jews of Wall Street' for ruining America. Germany's Jewish population had made no effective move to rebuff his anti-Semitism (anti-Jewish racism); it was as if, by not confronting Hitler, they hoped he would go away. "

Gordon Thomas and Max Morgan-Witts, in The Day the Bubble Burst: A Social History of the Wall Street Crash, *1979.*

Hitler at a Nazi rally in Dortmund in the 1930s. The misery caused by the economic slump led to a dramatic increase in support for the Nazis.

Could the Wall Street Crash have been avoided? Speculative manias, once they get going, gather their own momentum. They become increasingly difficult to stop, except by a crash. Usually those people who have the power to end the mania are the very people most caught up in the frenzy.

This was certainly the case in the speculative era between 1924 and 1929. The men who had the resources or the reputations to dampen the fever – such as Charles E Mitchell, John J Raskob and Richard A Whitney – were all committed to the boom in a personal way. They had staked their own fortunes on it continuing, so they were hardly likely to try to bring it to an end.

The men of the Federal Reserve Board (FRB) were certainly aware of the dangers of a crash in early 1929. They could have asked Congress for the power to set margin requirements, restricting the amount of money people could borrow to buy shares. If they had done this and warned people of the dangers of such reckless speculation on the stock-market, they might have prevented the crash. The bubble might have deflated rather than burst. Unfortunately, the FRB at this time were, in the words of economic historian J K Galbraith, 'a body of startling incompetence'. None of them wished to risk their careers and reputations by bringing the boom to a premature end. They feared that by speaking out too loudly they might themselves bring about a major crash, so they remained silent.

But what if they had acted, and the Wall Street Crash of October 1929 had never happened? How different might history have been? There would have been no banking crisis, no sudden urgency to recall all foreign debt, no large-scale bankruptcies and business closures. The world was certainly heading for an economic recession at that time. But without the crash, we would probably not be looking back on the 1930s as a time of such extreme unemployment, poverty and hardship.

The Federal Bank of New York, one of twelve federal banks across the USA, took the lead in lowering interest rates in 1927, encouraging the frenzy of speculation that led to the crash. The Federal Reserve Board, which oversaw the nation's banking, failed to react.

A Moment in Time

There is a crowd gathered in the visitors' gallery on 24 October 1929, to witness the mayhem on the floor of the New York Stock Exchange. Among them is Winston Churchill, the future wartime prime minister of Britain. As he watches the panic on the Stock Exchange floor, does Churchill consider his own part in bringing it about?

In the 1920s, as Chancellor of the Exchequer, Churchill had pursued a policy that led to a rise in the value of the pound against the dollar. This made Britain a less attractive place to buy and invest than the USA. So, in 1927 Britain pleaded with the FRB to lower interest rates in the USA, to even things up between the two countries. The FRB obliged, and by doing so sparked the boom and speculative fever that led to the crash.

Winston Churchill during a visit to the USA in 1929. He departed the country a little poorer, after witnessing his stock decline in value in the crash.

A normal recession might not have generated the violent social and political upheaval in Europe which allowed the Nazis to rise to power in Germany. Without a Nazi government, there would probably have been no German military aggression in the latter 1930s. This might even have prevented the Second World War, with all its many consequences for the rest of the twentieth century. This is not to suggest that a world war would not have happened without the crash. Other events might have led to it, such as the Nazis seizing power in Germany by force. But it is fair to say that the Wall Street Crash made it more likely.

A despairing broker during Black Monday 1987, when the stock-market lost nearly a quarter of its value in one day.

FOR THIRTY YEARS AFTER the Wall Street Crash, nearly all but the wealthiest Americans stopped speculating on the stock-market. But as the years went by, memories blurred. Government controls were now in place to try to prevent another crash occurring. New generations, unscarred by the crash, began to come into the market.

The speculative mood has returned on several occasions since 1929, most notably when it led to a crash on 19 October 1987. That day witnessed the largest stock-market fall to that time, when the industrial average plunged 508 points. The crash marked the end of a five-year bull market that had seen the industrial average rise from 776 points in August 1982 to 2,722 points in August 1987. Unlike Black Tuesday in 1929, Black Monday in 1987 did not have such a dramatic effect. This time, the Federal Reserve Board acted decisively to lend cash where needed, and to buy up stocks, so that banks and businesses affected by the crash did not go bankrupt. The market recovered quickly, and by September 1989 had regained all the value lost in the crash.

The stock-market crashed again in 2000, in a similar event to that of 1929, although this time only one sort of stock was affected. Both crashes were preceded by ten years of relative prosperity and an ever-rising bull market. In both eras there was talk of an exciting new technology. It was radio in the 1920s. In the 1990s,

it was the Internet, and a mania worthy of the 1920s took place. Everyone raced to invest in 'dot-coms' – companies that traded on the Internet – even though most of them were making losses. Even when the share prices of several leading dot-coms collapsed in the spring of 2000, investors were not put off. By the summer the bubble had grown so big that a relatively unknown dot-com like Corvis was briefly worth more than General Motors. Another big fall came in the

A trader on the floor of the NYSE during the dot-com bubble of 2000.

autumn, wiping out more than $3 trillion in stock-market value – enough to destroy the fortunes of many small investors. The collapse of the dot-com sector in 2000 was a major cause of the worldwide economic slowdown in 2001.

The weakness of the stock-market, and any process that tempts people to buy on the promise of prosperity, remains the same. All speculative eras begin with a rational opportunity. Yet it is easy to see how, as investors rush to take advantage, share prices can be pushed up to a level where they no longer reflect a company's worth. The richer people become by this process, the less they will want to see the dangers, and the more they will believe that the market will continue to rise. It happened in a big way on Wall Street in 1929, and it will happen again.

The Technology Bubble of 2000

In every speculative mania there is always the belief that this time it will be different, this time it cannot fail. In 2000, the lessons of 1929 were ignored or dismissed as irrelevant. Americans invested a total of $330 billion in dot-coms. Just as in 1929, supply in the technology market had outstripped demand. Prices for Internet access plunged, as they did for mobile phones – the other fashionable technology of the era. Share prices fell dramatically in April, in October, and once again in December.

The New York Stock Exchange on 17 September 2001, the first day of trading since two hijacked airliners crashed into the World Trade Center on 11 September. Following the attack, the industrial average plummeted a record 684 points. The exchange was forced to close, and by the following weekend three years of gains had been wiped out.

Glossary

assets A person's or company's property.

balanced budget A situation where the amount a country spends is equal to its income.

bankrupted Financially ruined, and unable to pay debts.

bear market A situation in which the majority of share prices are falling.

brokers Brokers, or stockbrokers, are people who buy and sell shares on behalf of investors.

bull market A situation in which the majority of share prices are rising.

capitalism A system in which trade and industry are controlled by private owners for profit.

common stocks Another word for shares.

communists People who believe in a system where the state controls property, trade and production.

Congress The place where the laws of the USA are debated and passed.

consumer goods Items bought by people for domestic use, e.g. cars and washing machines.

democracy A type of government where power rests with the people.

Democratic Party One of the two main political parties in the USA.

dividend A share of a business's profit paid to a shareholder.

Dow Jones The Dow Jones Index is the main indicator of trends and prices of shares on the US stock-market.

easy credit When the cost of borrowing is low.

economic depression A long period when trade is very slow, marked by high unemployment and poverty.

fascists People who support a national movement that is authoritarian and has control over the economy and individual freedoms.

import taxes Taxes paid by those who wish to sell goods to another country. Also known as *tariffs*.

industrial average The average value of shares of the top thirty companies on the Stock Exchange – a good indicator of the performance of the stock-market.

infrastructure The basic framework of a country that allows it to function, especially its transport network.

instalment plan A way of buying expensive goods by paying for them in stages rather than all at once.

interest rates The variable rate at which a bank charges people for borrowing money. This therefore controls the cost of borrowing.

investment trust (IT) A company that uses its money to invest in the shares of other companies.

margin call A demand made to a share-buyer for more cash to support an investment. This occurs when the shares that have been bought with borrowed money drop below a certain value and can no longer act as a guarantee for the loan.

margin requirements In margin trading, this is the percentage of the share price that must be paid for in cash (with the rest of the price paid for by the loan).

margin trading Buying shares by means of a part-payment in cash, the shares themselves acting as a guarantee for the loan.

market Short for *stock-market*.

mortgaged Offered as security (e.g. a house) in return for a loan.

nationalism Loyalty and devotion to your nation. In its extreme form this can also be a belief that your nation is better than other nations.

on margin Buying shares *on margin* means putting down a cash deposit for them and borrowing the remainder.

organized support The group of senior bankers who agreed to pool their resources and try to stabilize the plunging New York stock-market in October 1929.

pneumatic Working by means of air pressure.

points When refering to share prices on the New York stock-market, points mean dollars.